2011 year planner

	JULY	AUGUST	SEPTEMBER	OCTOBER	NOVEMBER	DECEMBER
MON		1				
TUE		2				
WED		3				
THU		4	1			
FRI	1	5	2			
SAT	2	6	3	1		
SUN	3	7	4	2	6	4
MON	4	8	5	3	7	5
TUE	5	9	6	4	8	6
WED	6	10	7	5	9	7
THU	7	11	8	6	10	8
FRI	8	12	9	7	11	9
SAT	9	13	10	8	12	10
SUN	10	14	11	9	13	11
MON	11	15	12	10	14	12
TUE	12	16	13	11	15	13
WED	13	17	14	12	16	14
THU	14	18	15	13	17	15
FRI	15	19	16	14	18	16
SAT	16	20	17	15	19	17
SUN	17	21	18	16	20	18
MON	18	22	19	17	21	19
TUE	19	23	20	18	22	20
WED	20	24	21	19	23	21
THU	21	25	22	20	24	22
FRI	22	26	23	21	25	23
SAT	23	27	24	22	26	24
SUN	24	28	25	23	27	25
MON	25	29	26	24	28	26
TUE	26	30	27	25	29	27
WED	27	31	28	26	30	28
THU	28		29	27		29
FRI	29		30	28		30
SAT	30			29		31
SUN	31			30		
MON				31		
TUE						

A LITTLE BIT ABOUT US...

Amnesty International

We are ordinary people from across the world standing up for humanity and human rights. Our purpose is to protect individuals wherever justice, fairness, freedom and truth are denied.

For further information contact:

IN BRITAIN:
Amnesty International
United Kingdom
The Human Rights
Action Centre
17-25 New Inn Yard
London EC2A 3EA
Tel +44 (0) 20 7033 1500

IN IRELAND:
Amnesty International
Ireland
Ballast House
First Floor
18-21 Westmoreland Street
Dublin 2 Ireland
Tel +353 (0) 1 863 83 00

IN THE NETHERLANDS:
Amnesty International
Netherlands
Keizersgracht 177
1016 DR Amsterdam
Tel +31 20 626 44 36

2010

January
M	T	W	T	F	S	S
				1	2	3
4	5	6	7	8	9	10
11	12	13	14	15	16	17
18	19	20	21	22	23	24
25	26	27	28	29	30	31

February
M	T	W	T	F	S	S
1	2	3	4	5	6	7
8	9	10	11	12	13	14
15	16	17	18	19	20	21
22	23	24	25	26	27	28

March
M	T	W	T	F	S	S
1	2	3	4	5	6	7
8	9	10	11	12	13	14
15	16	17	18	19	20	21
22	23	24	25	26	27	28
29	30	31				

April
M	T	W	T	F	S	S
			1	2	3	4
5	6	7	8	9	10	11
12	13	14	15	16	17	18
19	20	21	22	23	24	25
26	27	28	29	30		

May
M	T	W	T	F	S	S
					1	2
3	4	5	6	7	8	9
10	11	12	13	14	15	16
17	18	19	20	21	22	23
24	25	26	27	28	29	30
31						

June
M	T	W	T	F	S	S
	1	2	3	4	5	6
7	8	9	10	11	12	13
14	15	16	17	18	19	20
21	22	23	24	25	26	27
28	29	30				

July
M	T	W	T	F	S	S
			1	2	3	4
5	6	7	8	9	10	11
12	13	14	15	16	17	18
19	20	21	22	23	24	25
26	27	28	29	30	31	

August
M	T	W	T	F	S	S
						1
2	3	4	5	6	7	8
9	10	11	12	13	14	15
16	17	18	19	20	21	22
23	24	25	26	27	28	29
30	31					

September
M	T	W	T	F	S	S
		1	2	3	4	5
6	7	8	9	10	11	12
13	14	15	16	17	18	19
20	21	22	23	24	25	26
27	28	29	30			

October
M	T	W	T	F	S	S
				1	2	3
4	5	6	7	8	9	10
11	12	13	14	15	16	17
18	19	20	21	22	23	24
25	26	27	28	29	30	31

November
M	T	W	T	F	S	S
1	2	3	4	5	6	7
8	9	10	11	12	13	14
15	16	17	18	19	20	21
22	23	24	25	26	27	28
29	30					

December
M	T	W	T	F	S	S
		1	2	3	4	5
6	7	8	9	10	11	12
13	14	15	16	17	18	19
20	21	22	23	24	25	26
27	28	29	30	31		

2012

January
M	T	W	T	F	S	S
						1
2	3	4	5	6	7	8
9	10	11	12	13	14	15
16	17	18	19	20	21	22
23	24	25	26	27	28	29
30	31					

February
M	T	W	T	F	S	S
		1	2	3	4	5
6	7	8	9	10	11	12
13	14	15	16	17	18	19
20	21	22	23	24	25	26
27	28	29				

March
M	T	W	T	F	S	S
			1	2	3	4
5	6	7	8	9	10	11
12	13	14	15	16	17	18
19	20	21	22	23	24	25
26	27	28	29	30	31	

April
M	T	W	T	F	S	S
						1
2	3	4	5	6	7	8
9	10	11	12	13	14	15
16	17	18	19	20	21	22
23	24	25	26	27	28	29
30						

May
M	T	W	T	F	S	S
	1	2	3	4	5	6
7	8	9	10	11	12	13
14	15	16	17	18	19	20
21	22	23	24	25	26	27
28	29	30	31			

June
M	T	W	T	F	S	S
				1	2	3
4	5	6	7	8	9	10
11	12	13	14	15	16	17
18	19	20	21	22	23	24
25	26	27	28	29	30	

July
M	T	W	T	F	S	S
						1
2	3	4	5	6	7	8
9	10	11	12	13	14	15
16	17	18	19	20	21	22
23	24	25	26	27	28	29
30	31					

August
M	T	W	T	F	S	S
		1	2	3	4	5
6	7	8	9	10	11	12
13	14	15	16	17	18	19
20	21	22	23	24	25	26
27	28	29	30	31		

September
M	T	W	T	F	S	S
					1	2
3	4	5	6	7	8	9
10	11	12	13	14	15	16
17	18	19	20	21	22	23
24	25	26	27	28	29	30

October
M	T	W	T	F	S	S
1	2	3	4	5	6	7
8	9	10	11	12	13	14
15	16	17	18	19	20	21
22	23	24	25	26	27	28
29	30	31				

November
M	T	W	T	F	S	S
			1	2	3	4
5	6	7	8	9	10	11
12	13	14	15	16	17	18
19	20	21	22	23	24	25
26	27	28	29	30		

December
M	T	W	T	F	S	S
					1	2
3	4	5	6	7	8	9
10	11	12	13	14	15	16
17	18	19	20	21	22	23
24	25	26	27	28	29	30
31						

personal info

Name
....

Address
....

....

Phone
....

Mobile
....

College/Work Address
....

....

Passport Number
....

National Insurance Number
....

Doctor
....

Dentist
....

In case of an emergency
....

Name
....

Address
....

....

Phone
....

Mobile
....

....

....

....

....

get active!

HUMAN RIGHTS

Action Aid
www.actionaid.org

Amnesty International
www.amnesty.org

Anti-Slavery International
www.antislavery.org

Article 19 (freedom of expression/information)
www.article19.org

Assembly of First Nations (Canada)
www.afn.ca

Australians for Native Title and Reconciliation (ANTaR)
www.antar.org.au

AVAAZ
www.avaaz.org

Disabled Peoples International
www.dpi.org

Egale Canada (LGBT)
www.egale.ca

First Peoples Worldwide
www.firstpeoples.org

Global Call to Action Against Poverty
www.whiteband.org

Global Witness
www.globalwitness.org

Human Rights Watch
www.hrw.org

Indigenous Environment Network
www.ienearth.org

Interights
www.interights.org

International P.E.N./Writers in Prison Committee
www.internationalpen.org.uk

International Centre for Rights and Democracy
www.dd-rd.ca

International Lesbian and Gay Association
www.ilga.org

Jubilee Debt Campaign
www.jubileedebtcampaign.org.uk

Liberty
www.liberty-human-rights.org.uk

Médecins sans Frontières (MSF)
www.msf.org

Minority Rights Group (MRG)
www.minorityrights.org

New Matilda
www.humanrightsact.com.au

Oxfam International
www.oxfaminternational.org

People's Movement for Human Rights Education
www.pdhre.org

Project Respect
www.projectrespect.org.au

Rights Australia
www.rightsaustralia.org.au

Rural Australians for Refugees
www.ruralaustraliansforrefugees.org

Stonewall UK (LGBT)
www.stonewall.org.uk

Survival
www.survival-international.org

Via Campesina
viacampesina.org

Womenaid International
www.womenaid.org

Working Abroad
www.workingabroad.com

get active!

ENVIRONMENT/CLIMATE CHANGE

Art Not Oil
www.artnotoil.org.uk

Camp for Climate Action
www.climatecamp.org.uk

Carbon Trade Watch
www.carbontradewatch.org

Climate Action Network
www.climatenetwork.org

Climate Indymedia
www.climateimc.org

The Corner House
www.thecornerhouse.org.uk/
subject/climate/

David Suzuki Foundation
www.davidsuzuki.org

Dirty Oil Sands
www.dirtyoilsands.org

Energy Action Coalition
www.energyaction.net

Environmental Defence
www.environmentaldefence.ca

Focus on Global South
http://focusweb.org

Friends of the Earth
www.foei.org

Global Campaign for Climate Action
http://gc-ca.org

Global Justice Ecology Project
www.globaljusticeecology.org

Greenpeace International
www.greenpeace.org

Indigenous Environment Network
www.ienearth.org

Mining Watch Canada
www.miningwatch.ca

Oil Sands Truth
http://oilsandstruth.org

Oilwatch International
www.oilwatch.org

People & Planet
http://peopleandplanet.org

Planet Ark
www.planetark.org

Platform
www.platformlondon.org

Rainforest Action Network
www.ran.org

Real Climate
www.realclimate.org

Rising Tide North America
www.risingtidenorthamerica.org

Rising Tide Aotearoa/NZ
www.risingtide.org.nz

Rising Tide Australia
http://risingtide.org.au

Rising Tide UK
http://risingtide.org.uk

Sierra Club (US)
www.sierraclub.org

Stop Climate Chaos
www.stopclimatechaos.org

350°
www.350.org

World Rainforest Movement
www.wrm.org.uy

PEACE/ARMS TRADE

Arms Trade Resource Center (US)
www.worldpolicy.org/projects/
arms

Australian Campaign Against Arms Trade
www.acaat.org

Campaign Against Arms Trade (UK)
www.caat.org.uk

get active!

Campagne Tegen
Wapenhandel (Netherlands)
www.antenna.nl/amokmar

Ceasefire (South Africa)
stopwar@wn.apc.org

Coalition to Oppose the Arms Trade (Canada)
www.ncf.carleton.ca

Canadian Peace Alliance
www.acp-cpa.ca

Centre for Conflict Resolution (South Africa)
http://ccrweb.ccr.uct.ac.za

The Centre for Peace Studies (Australia)
http://fehps.une.edu.au/PDaL/
Courses/ProfessionalStudies/
peace/

European Network Against Arms Trade
www.antenna.nl/enaat

International Action Network on Small Arms
www.iansa.org

International Campaign to Ban Landmines
www.icbl.org

Landmine Action
www.landmineaction.org

Nuke Watch
www.nukewatch.org.uk
www.nukewatch.com

Peace Movement Aotearoa
www.converge.org.nz/pma/

Saferworld UK
www.saferworld.org.uk

Stockholm International Peace Research Institute
www.sipri.org

United Nations peace website
www.un.org/peace/

TRADE JUSTICE

AFTINET (Australia)
www.aftinet.org.au

Buy Nothing Day
www.buynothingday.co.uk

Campaigns against supermarket expansion:
www.tescopoly.org.uk

Corporate Watch
www.corporatewatch.org

Ethical Consumer magazine
www.ethicalconsumer.org

The Fairtrade Labeling Organizations International
www.fairtrade.net

Freecycle Network Free exchanges
www.freecycle.org

Global Trade Watch
www.citizen.org/trade/

The International Fair Trade Association
www.ifat.org

Make Poverty History
www.makepovertyhistory.org

The Trade Justice Movement
www.tjm.org.uk

Wake-up Wal-Mart
www.wakeupwalmart.com

dates and holidays

Sat 1 January	New Year's Day
Mon 17 January	Martin Luther King Day (US)
Thurs 3 February	Chinese New Year
Sun 6 February	Waitangi Day (NZ)
Mon 14 February	St Valentine's Day
Tues 15 February	Nirvana Day (Buddhist, Jain); Mawlid an Nabi (Islam)
Mon 21 February	Presidents' Day (US)
Tue 8 March	International Women's Day
Sun 13 March	Clocks change (N. America)
Thu 17 March	St Patrick's Day (Ire)
Tue 22 March	World Day for Water
Sun 27 March	Clocks change (UK)
Fri 1 April	April Fools' Day
Sun 3 April	Clocks change (NZ/Aus)
Mon 4 April	New Year (Hindu)
Thu 7 April	World Health Day
Tue 19 April	Pesach (Jewish)
Fri 22 April	Good Friday
Sun 24 April	Easter
Mon 25 April	Easter Monday/Anzac Day (NZ)
Tue 26 April	Anzac Day (Australia)
Mon 2 May	Early May Bank Holiday (UK)
Tue 3 May	World Press Freedom Day
Sat 14 May	World Fair Trade Day
Tue 17 May	Buddha Day
Mon 23 May	Victoria Day (Can)
Mon 30 May	Spring Bank Holiday (UK), Memorial Day (US)
Tue 31 May	World No Tobacco Day
Sun 5 June	World Environment Day
Mon 6 June	Queen's Birthday (NZ)
Wed 8 June	Shavuot (Jewish)
Mon 13 June	Queen's Birthday (Aus)
Fri 1 July	Canada Day (Can)
Mon 4 July	Independence Day (US)
Mon 1 August	Summer Bank Holiday (Scot), Civic holiday (Can), Ramadan begins (Islam)
Tues 9 August	World's Indigenous Peoples' Day
Mon 29 August	Summer Bank Holiday (UK except Scotland)
Tues 30 August	Eid al Fitr (Islam)
Mon 5 September	Labour Day (Canada), Labor Day (US)
Sun 25 September	Clocks change (NZ)
Thu 29 September	Rosh Hashanah (Jewish)
Sun 2 October	Clocks change (Aus)
Mon 3 October	Labour Day (Aus)
Sat 8 October	Yom Kippur (Jewish)
Mon 10 October	Thanksgiving (Canada), Columbus Day (US)
Thu 13 October	Sukkot (Jewish)
Mon 24 October	Labour Day (NZ)
Wed 26 October	Diwali (Jain, Hindu, Sikh)
Sun 30 October	Clocks change (UK))
Mon 31 October	Hallowe'en
Sat 5 November	Guy Fawkes Night
Sun 6 November	Clocks change (N. America)
Fri 11 November	Remembrance Day (Canada), Veterans' Day (US)
Thu 24 November	Thanksgiving (US)
Sat 26 November	Islamic New Year
Thu 1 December	World AIDS Day
Wed 21 December	Hanukah (Jewish)
Sun 25 December	Christmas Day
Mon 26 December	Public holiday (UK, US, Aus, Can, NZ)
Tue 27 December	Public holiday (UK, Aus, NZ)

"Most people are about as happy as they make up their minds to be."
— Abraham Lincoln (1809-1865), US President

The Emperor
Kate Charlesworth
www.katecharlesworth.com

JANUARY

2010

Public holiday, UK, Aus, Can, NZ **MONDAY** 27

Public holiday, UK, Aus, Can, NZ **TUESDAY** 28

WEDNESDAY 29

THURSDAY 30

New Year's Eve **FRIDAY** 31

2011

New Year's Day **SATURDAY** 1

SUNDAY 2

JANUARY

3 MONDAY New Year's Day holiday (UK, Aus, Can)

· ·

4 TUESDAY Holiday (Scotland, NZ)

· ·

5 WEDNESDAY

· ·

6 THURSDAY

· ·

7 FRIDAY

· ·

8 SATURDAY

· ·

9 SUNDAY

· ·

Green, Green Gas of Home
Kate Charlesworth
www.katecharlesworth.com

JANUARY

MONDAY 10

TUESDAY 11

WEDNESDAY 12

THURSDAY 13

FRIDAY 14

SATURDAY 15

SUNDAY 16

JANUARY

17 MONDAY Martin Luther King Day (US)

· ·

18 TUESDAY

· ·

19 WEDNESDAY

· ·

20 THURSDAY

· ·

21 FRIDAY

· ·

22 SATURDAY

· ·

23 SUNDAY

· ·

JANUARY

MONDAY 24

....

TUESDAY 25

....

WEDNESDAY 26

....

THURSDAY 27

....

FRIDAY 28

....

SATURDAY 29

....

SUNDAY 30

....

JANUARY

31   MONDAY

· ·

I've created strips, cartoons and illustrations for a wide-ranging client list (see www.katecharlesworth.com). and have a particular interest in LGBT and women's issues, science, ecology and the natural world.

Kate Charlesworth

FEBRUARY

Tuesday 1

....

Wednesday 2

....

Chinese New Year Thursday 3

....

Friday 4

....

Saturday 5

....

Waitangi Day (NZ) Sunday 6

....

FEBRUARY

7   Monday

....

8   Tuesday

....

9   Wednesday

....

10   Thursday

....

11   Friday

....

12   Saturday

....

13   Sunday

....

MAKE CARBON HISTORY?

Make carbon history?
Steve Stuffit
www.stuffit.org

bp solar

energy independence
For your home, for your business, for your country.

Virgin

383
F-WW

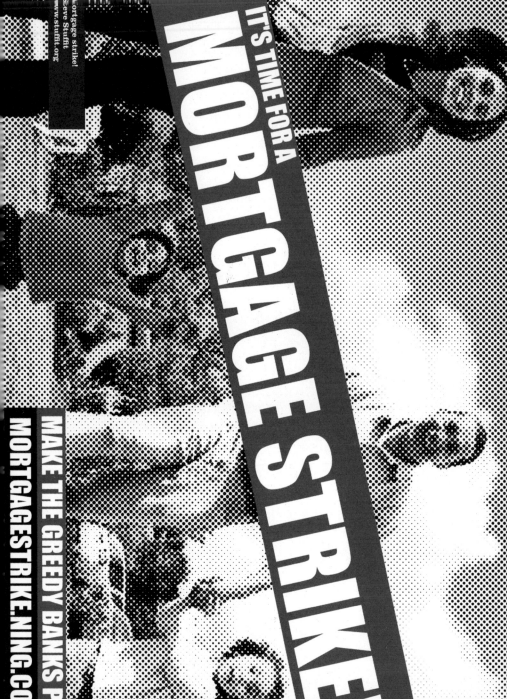

IT'S TIME FOR A
MORTGAGE STRIKE!

Mortgage strike!
Steve Stuffit
www.stuffit.org

MAKE THE GREEDY BANKS PAY
MORTGAGESTRIKE.NING.COM

FEBRUARY

St Valentine's Day **Monday** 14

Nirvana Day (Buddhist, Jain); Mawlid an Nabi (Islam) **Tuesday** 15

Wednesday 16

Thursday 17

Friday 18

Saturday 19

Sunday 20

FEBRUARY

21 Monday Presidents' Day (US)

22 Tuesday

23 Wednesday

24 Thursday

25 Friday

26 Saturday

27 Sunday

All that's solid melts into air

YOU CAN'T OFFSET

A SOCIAL RELATIONSHIP

CO2 CO2 CO2 CO2 CO2 CO2

WWW.STUFFIT.C

You can't offset a social relationship
Steve Stuffit
www.stuffit.org

FEBRUARY

Steve Stuffit is a Bristol-based ecological artist who makes books, postcards, fanzines, texts, screenprints, videos, websites and nettle beer about class war and the environment. As well as making art, Mr Stuffit likes to work and collaborate with East Bristol Debtors Alliance (www.eb-da.org), the IWW union (www.iww.org.uk), Bristol Radical History Group (www.brh.org.uk) and Bristol Anarchist Bookfair Collective (www.bristolanarchistbookfair.org.uk). He is also interested in permaculture and shares an allotment with his partner and some friends. All the work is documented and available for download and participation at www.stuffit.org

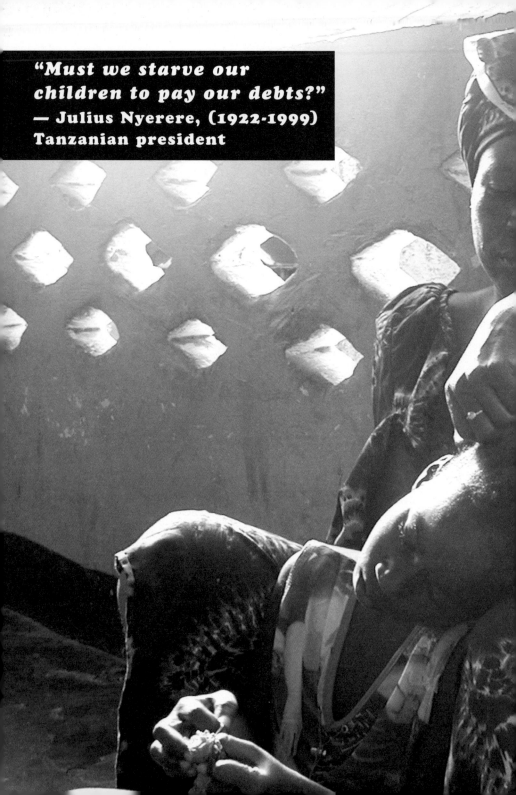

"Must we starve our children to pay our debts?"
— Julius Nyerere, (1922-1999)
Tanzanian president

MARCH

1   TUESDAY

. . . .

2   WEDNESDAY

. . . .

3   THURSDAY

. . . .

4   FRIDAY

. . . .

5   SATURDAY

. . . .

6   SUNDAY

. . . .

Urban Jungle – One Day in
the Life of a Business Man
Kathryn Spreadbury
www.kathrynspreadbury.co.uk

Urban Jungle – One Day in
the Life of a Business Man
Kathryn Spreadbury
www.kathrynspreadbury.co.uk

MARCH

MONDAY   7

....

International Women's Day   TUESDAY   8

....

WEDNESDAY   9

....

THURSDAY   10

....

FRIDAY   11

....

SATURDAY   12

....

Clocks change (N. America)   SUNDAY   13

....

MARCH

14 MONDAY
· ·

15 TUESDAY
· ·

16 WEDNESDAY
· ·

17 THURSDAY St Patrick's Day (Ire)
· ·

18 FRIDAY
· ·

19 SATURDAY
· ·

20 SUNDAY
· ·

**Urban Jungle – One Day in
the Life of a Business Man
Kathryn Spreadbury
www.kathrynspreadbury.co.uk**

MARCH

MONDAY 21

....

World Day for Water **TUESDAY** 22

....

WEDNESDAY 23

....

THURSDAY 24

....

FRIDAY 25

....

SATURDAY 26

....

Clocks change (UK) **SUNDAY** 27

....

MARCH

28 MONDAY

. . . .

29 TUESDAY

. . . .

30 WEDNESDAY

. . . .

31 THURSDAY

. . . .

Kathryn Spreadbury was inspired by visiting Canary Wharf in London and doing observational drawings, which sparked her to write a narrative 'Urban Jungle' that then became the backbone of creating her images. This particular image is part of the series. Kathryn wanted to exaggerate the dark, depressing views of a nine-to-five job, to give her characters not much expression and to hint at repetitiveness as well as her views of business. In this image she wanted to exaggerate this dark, dominating figure of a big boss towering over his employees. Kathryn likes to use a wide variety of media in her work, including charcoal and ink, which she used to create this dark, dirty atmosphere. She graduated from UCA Maidstone in 2009 and is currently living and working in Maidstone, Kent.

Urban Jungle – One Day in
the Life of a Business Man
Kathryn Spreadbury
www.kathrynspreadbury.co.uk

A409 CLOSED AT BAMPTON FOLLOW DIVERSION

Picnic table
Tara Lawfull
t.lawfull@gmail.com

APRIL

April Fools' Day **FRIDAY** 1

SATURDAY 2

Clocks change (NZ/AUS) **SUNDAY** 3

APRIL

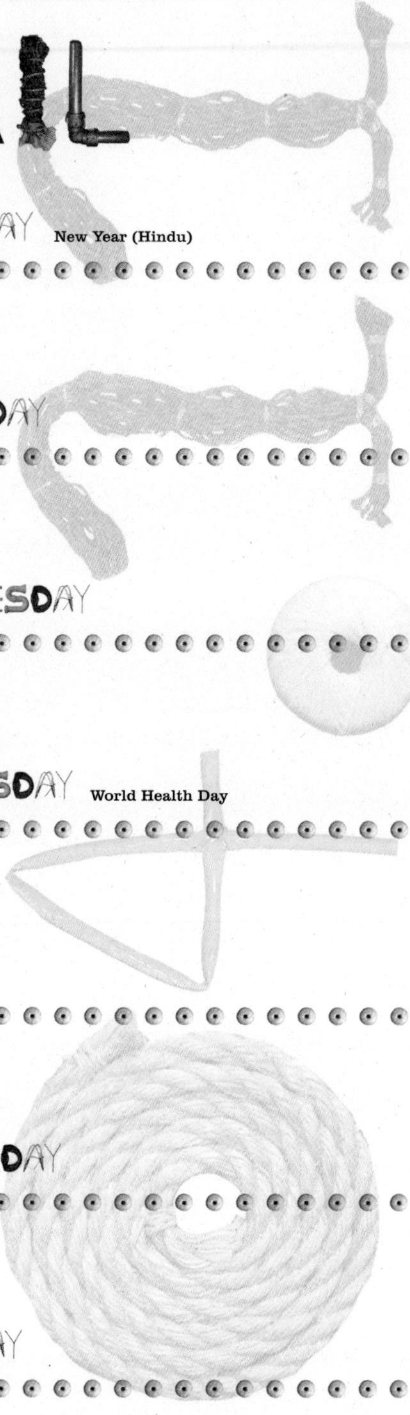

4   MONDAY   **New Year (Hindu)**

5   TUESDAY

6   WEDNESDAY

7   THURSDAY   **World Health Day**

8   FRIDAY

9   SATURDAY

10   SUNDAY

Metamorphosis of Junk
Tara Lawfull
t.lawfull@gmail.com

Metamorphosis of Junk
Tara Lawfull
t.lawfull@gmail.com

APRIL

MONDAY 11

TUESDAY 12

WEDNESDAY 13

THURSDAY 14

FRIDAY 15

SATURDAY 16

SUNDAY 17

APRIL

18 MONDAY

19 TUESDAY Pesach (Jewish)

20 WEDNESDAY

21 THURSDAY

22 FRIDAY Good Friday

23 SATURDAY

24 SUNDAY Easter

Metamorphosis of Junk
Tara Lawfull
t.lawfull@gmail.com

Metamorphosis of Junk
Tara Lawfull
t.lawfull@gmail.com

APRIL

MONDAY 25
Easter Monday/Anzac Day (NZ)

TUESDAY 26
Anzac Day (Aus)

WEDNESDAY 27

THURSDAY 28

FRIDAY 29

SATURDAY 30

I have always been motivated by concerns about the environment and have enjoyed expressing this through my work. I focus on re-cycling junk. I like to understand it as a visual communication between junk and art similar to an ocular language. Concentrating mainly on the physical shape, form and structure of an object. I explore the qualities of an object through their characteristics and significant value, by understanding the transformation whereby a piece of junk can exit the junk pile to become something useful again.

Tara Lawfull

"There is no wealth but life."
— John Ruskin (1819-1908),
British artist

MAY

05

1 SUNDAY

The Sprawl
John Ledger
www.johnledgerartist.com

MAY

MONDAY 2

Early May Bank Holiday (UK)

• •

TUESDAY 3

World Press Freedom Day

• •

WEDNESDAY 4

• •

THURSDAY $\overline{5}$

• •

FRIDAY $\overline{6}$

• •

SATURDAY 7

• •

SUNDAY $\overline{8}$

• •

9 MONDAY

10 TUESDAY

11 WEDNESDAY

12 THURSDAY

13 FRIDAY

14 SATURDAY World Fair Trade Day

15 SUNDAY

Global pillage
John Ledger
www.johnledgerartist.com

MAY

MONDAY `16`

Buddha Day   **TUESDAY** `17`

WEDNESDAY `18`

THURSDAY `19`

FRIDAY `20`

SATURDAY `21`

SUNDAY `22`

MAY

23 MONDAY   Victoria Day (Can)

24 TUESDAY

25 WEDNESDAY

26 THURSDAY

27 FRIDAY

28 SATURDAY   On this day in 1961 Amnesty International was created.

29 SUNDAY

The alpha forest
John Ledger
www.johnledgerartist.com

A frog in warming water (just a myth)
John Ledger
www.johnledgerartist.com

MAY

Spring Bank Holiday (UK), Memorial Day (US) MONDAY 30

World No Tobacco Day TUESDAY 31

My artistic output is the only resistance I can put up against the feelings of hopelessness as I peer into the 21st century. Without my one method of resistance I would slip into a swamp of apathy and despair. My doodles, my only method of retaliation, turn into murals as I try to match the size of the oppressor. Consumer Capitalism renders everything and everybody pointless and worthless, whilst pampering our primitive requirements enough to pacify us, but sending us into environmental hell. My generation cannot rely on obtaining the domestic comforts our parents may have enjoyed. We have to perceive another type of world, one which isn't about getting the ideal home, ideal job or career; else we might as well build all our roads leading towards the cliff's edge.

John Ledger

JUNE

1 WEDNESDAY
....

2 THURSDAY
....

3 FRIDAY
....

4 SATURDAY
....

5 SUNDAY World Environment Day
....

Nothing I could see could bring me joy

JUNE

Queen's Birthday (NZ) MONDAY 6

···

TUESDAY 7

···

Shavuot (Jewish) WEDNESDAY 8

···

THURSDAY 9

···

FRIDAY 10

···

SATURDAY 11

···

SUNDAY 12

···

JUNE

13 MONDAY Queen's Birthday (Aus)

· ·

14 TUESDAY

· ·

15 WEDNESDAY

· ·

16 THURSDAY

· ·

17 FRIDAY

· ·

18 SATURDAY

· ·

19 SUNDAY

· ·

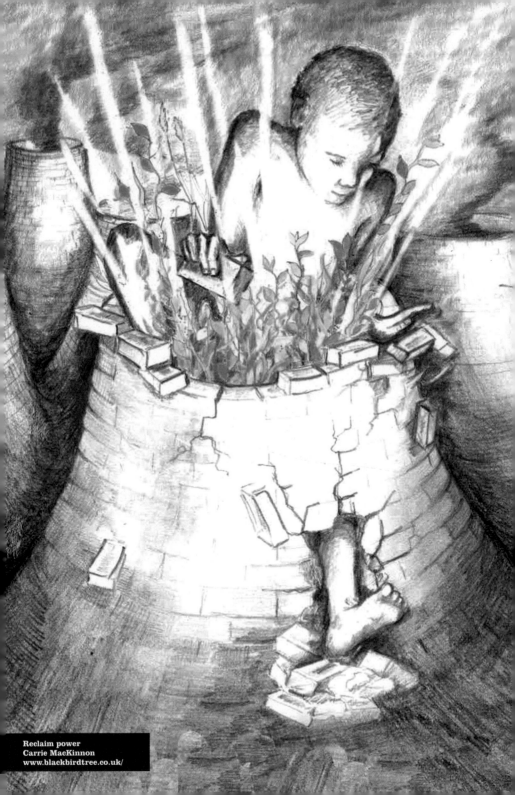

JUNE

MONDAY 20

....

TUESDAY 21

....

WEDNESDAY 22

....

THURSDAY 23

....

FRIDAY 24

....

SATURDAY 25

....

SUNDAY 26

....

JUNE

27 MONDAY

· ·

28 TUESDAY

· ·

29 WEDNESDAY

· ·

30 THURSDAY

· ·

**Carrie MacKinnon is an illustrator working from
her narrowboat home in Derbyshire, UK.**

The dream and the memory
Carrie MacKinnon
www.blackbirdtree.co.uk/

"Don't call me 'world music' – that's a neo-colonial label you British and Americans like to use for music not sung in English."
— Manu Chao, musician

JULY

Canada Day (Canada) **FRIDAY** 1

SATURDAY 2

SUNDAY 3

JULY

4 MONDAY Independence Day (US)

5 TUESDAY

6 WEDNESDAY

7 THURSDAY

8 FRIDAY

9 SATURDAY

10 SUNDAY

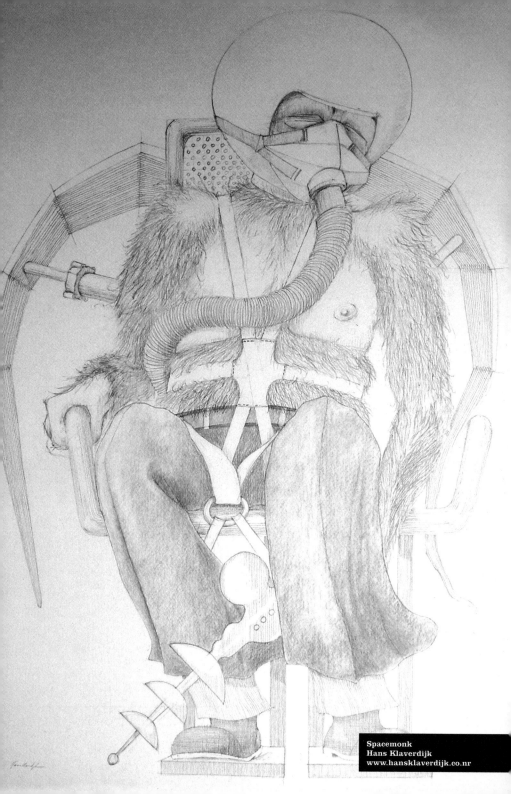

JULY

MONDAY 11

. . . .

TUESDAY 12

. . . .

WEDNESDAY 13

. . . .

THURSDAY 14

. . . .

FRIDAY 15

. . . .

SATURDAY 16

. . . .

SUNDAY 17

. . . .

JULY

18 MONDAY

· ·

19 TUESDAY

· ·

20 WEDNESDAY

· ·

21 THURSDAY

· ·

22 FRIDAY

· ·

23 SATURDAY

· ·

24 SUNDAY

· ·

JULY

MONDAY 25

··

TUESDAY 26

··

WEDNESDAY 27

··

THURSDAY 28

··

FRIDAY 29

··

SATURDAY 30

··

SUNDAY 31

··

Hans Klaverdijk is an illustrator based in Breda, Netherlands.

Pig
Andrew Wheatley
www.andrewwheatley.co.uk

AUGUST

Summer Bank Holiday (Scot), Civic holiday (Can),Ramadan begins (Islam) **MONDAY** 1

TUESDAY 2

WEDNESDAY 3

THURSDAY 4

FRIDAY 5

SATURDAY 6

SUNDAY 7

AUGUST

8   MONDAY

9   TUESDAY World's Indigenous Peoples' Day

10   WEDNESDAY

11   THURSDAY

12   FRIDAY

13   SATURDAY

14   SUNDAY

Week
Andrew Wheatley
www.andrewwheatley.co.uk

Snake
Andrew Wheatley
www.andrewwheatley.co.uk

AUGUST

MONDAY 15

. . . .

TUESDAY 16

. . . .

WEDNESDAY 17

. . . .

THURSDAY 18

. . . .

FRIDAY 19

. . . .

SATURDAY 20

. . . .

SUNDAY 21

. . . .

AUGUST

22   MONDAY

....

23   TUESDAY

....

24   WEDNESDAY

....

25   THURSDAY

....

26   FRIDAY

....

27   SATURDAY

....

28   SUNDAY

....

Time
Andrew Wheatley
www.andrewwheatley.co.uk

Mountain
Andrew Wheatley
www.andrewwheatley.co.uk

AUGUST

Summer Bank Holiday (UK except Scotland) **MONDAY** 29

Eid al Fitr (Islam) **TUESDAY** 30

WEDNESDAY 31

Andrew Wheatley is a freelance illustrator based in the UK. You can see more of his work at: www.andrewwheatley.co.uk.

"The question is not how to survive but how to thrive with passion, compassion, humour and style."
— Maya Angelou (1928-),
US writer

Dentist's kiosk
Pakistan
Andrew Kokotka

SEPTEMBER

1 THURSDAY

2 FRIDAY

3 SATURDAY

4 SUNDAY

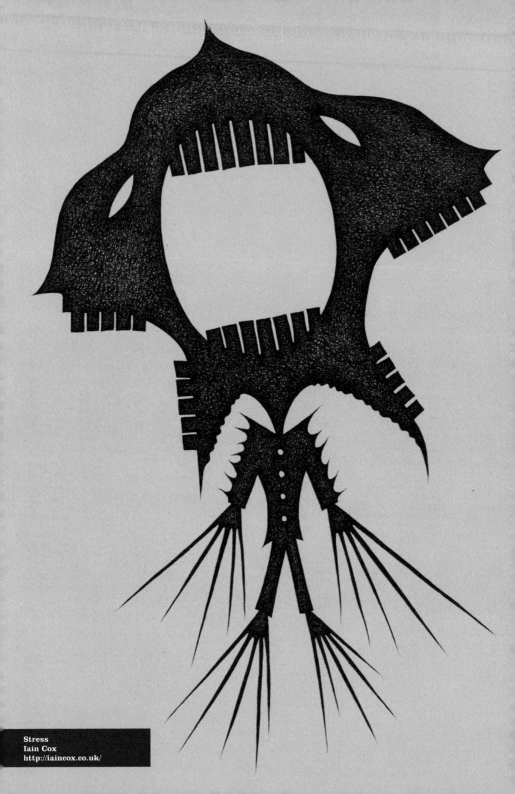

SEPTEMBER

Labour Day (Can), Labor Day (US) **MONDAY**   5

....

TUESDAY   6

....

WEDNESDAY   7

....

THURSDAY   8

....

FRIDAY   9

....

SATURDAY   10

....

SUNDAY   11

....

SEPTEMBER

12 MONDAY

13 TUESDAY

14 WEDNESDAY

15 THURSDAY

16 FRIDAY

17 SATURDAY

18 SUNDAY

The Dilemma
Iain Cox
http://iaincox.co.uk/

SEPTEMBER

MONDAY 19

. . . .

TUESDAY 20

. . . .

WEDNESDAY 21

. . . .

THURSDAY 22

. . . .

FRIDAY 23

. . . .

SATURDAY 24

. . . .

Clocks change (NZ) **SUNDAY 25**

. . . .

SEPTEMBER

26 MONDAY

· ·

27 TUESDAY

· ·

28 WEDNESDAY

· ·

29 THURSDAY Rosh Hashanah (Jewish)

· ·

30 FRIDAY

· ·

Iain Cox is an illustrator based in Maidstone, UK.

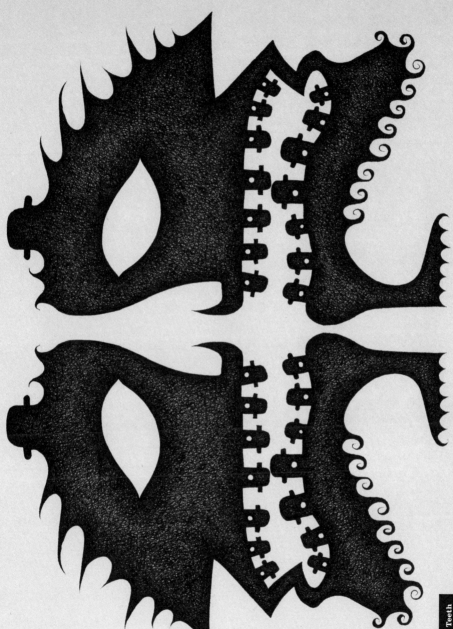

Commuter Series – Teeth
Iain Cox
http://iaincox.co.uk/

Farmers Markets
not
Carbon Markets

Climate Camp G20
Amelia Gregory
www.ameliasmagazine.com

OCTOBER

SATURDAY 1

Clocks change (Aus) SUNDAY 2

OCTOBER

3   MONDAY Labour Day (Aus)
....

4   TUESDAY
....

5   WEDNESDAY
....

6   THURSDAY
....

7   FRIDAY
....

8   SATURDAY Yom Kippur (Jewish)
....

9   SUNDAY
....

TAR SAND OIL IS BLOOD OIL

Climate Camp Tarsands Action
Amelia Gregory
www.ameliasmagazine.com

OCTOBER

Thanksgiving (Can), Columbus Day (US) MONDAY 10

TUESDAY 11

WEDNESDAY 12

Sukkot (Jewish) THURSDAY 13

FRIDAY 14

SATURDAY 15

SUNDAY 16

OCTOBER

17 MONDAY

18 TUESDAY

19 WEDNESDAY

20 THURSDAY

21 FRIDAY

22 SATURDAY

23 SUNDAY

BIKE LIBRARY
ASK US, TAKE IT, A LOCK
BRING IT BACK HERE.
— bikes then go to Calais SIMPLES.
for NoBorders group.

Climate Camp Ratcliffe Swoop
Amelia Gregory
www.ameliasmagazine.com

OCTOBER

Labour Day (NZ) MONDAY 24

. . . .

TUESDAY 25

. . . .

Diwali (Jain, Hindu, Sikh) WEDNESDAY 26

. . . .

THURSDAY 27

. . . .

FRIDAY 28

. . . .

SATURDAY 29

. . . .

Clocks change (UK) SUNDAY 30

. . . .

OCTOBER

31   MONDAY Hallowe'en

· ·

Amelia Gregory is an activist, photographer, blogger, publisher, editor and art director based in London. As part of Climate Camp she likes to document everything with a camera and via Twitter, using live video and audio streams. Whilst working as a fashion and music photographer she set up the arts and environment journal *Amelia's Magazine* in 2004, and is particularly interested in how creativity can be used to change the world. She has just published her first book, *Amelia's Anthology of Illustration* (featuring renewable technologies to prevent catastrophic climate change), which addresses how illustrators can help to imagine a positive future.

"Long live the unity of Latin America."
— Hugo Chavez (1954-), Venezuelan president

SIGLO XX

J.V. Gónez

OIL

EL CABITO

Venezuela
David Ransom
New Internationalist

NOVEMBER

1   **TUESDAY**
. . . .

2   **WEDNESDAY**
. . . .

3   **THURSDAY**
. . . .

4   **FRIDAY**
. . . .

5   **SATURDAY** Guy Fawkes Night
. . . .

6   **SUNDAY** Clocks change (N. America)
. . . .

NOVEMBER

MONDAY 7

TUESDAY 8

WEDNESDAY 9

THURSDAY 10

Remembrance Day (Can), Veterans' Day (US) **FRIDAY** 11

SATURDAY 12

SUNDAY 13

NOVEMBER

14 MONDAY

15 TUESDAY

16 WEDNESDAY

17 THURSDAY

18 FRIDAY

19 SATURDAY

20 SUNDAY

NOVEMBER

MONDAY 21

TUESDAY 22

WEDNESDAY 23

Thanksgiving (US) THURSDAY 24

FRIDAY 25

Islamic New Year SATURDAY 26

SUNDAY 27

NOVEMBER

28 MONDAY

29 TUESDAY

30 WEDNESDAY

Dario Utreras is an illustrator/photographer/designer based in London, UK.

I'm fat, look I'm fat
Robert Sae-Heng
www.sniffsniff.co.uk/

DECEMBER

World AIDS Day **THURSDAY** 1

· ·

FRIDAY 2

· ·

SATURDAY 3

· ·

SUNDAY 4

· ·

DECEMBER

5   **MONDAY**

· ·

6   **TUESDAY**

· ·

7   **WEDNESDAY**

· ·

8   **THURSDAY**

· ·

9   **FRIDAY**

· ·

10   **SATURDAY**

· ·

11   **SUNDAY**

· ·

She runs as if the sky were falling
Robert Sae-Heng
www.sniffsniff.co.uk/

DECEMBER

MONDAY 12

....

TUESDAY 13

....

WEDNESDAY 14

....

THURSDAY 15

....

FRIDAY 16

....

SATURDAY 17

....

SUNDAY 18

....

DECEMBER

19   MONDAY

20   TUESDAY

21   WEDNESDAY Hanukah (Jewish)

22   THURSDAY

23   FRIDAY

24   SATURDAY

25   SUNDAY Christmas Day

The eating thing
Robert Sae-Heng
www.sniffsniff.co.uk/

Anorexia and the media
Robert Sae-Heng
www.sniffsniff.co.uk/

DECEMBER

Public holiday (UK, US, Aus, Can, NZ) **MONDAY**   **26**

Public holiday (UK, Aus, NZ) **TUESDAY**   **27**

WEDNESDAY   **28**

THURSDAY   **29**

FRIDAY   **30**

New Year's Eve **SATURDAY**   **31**

2012   **SUNDAY**   **1**

I am an illustrator and designer based around the London area. I have an obsession for drawing and drinking warm Ribena. I was born deaf, but eventually learnt to read and speak. From an early age I found drawing as a way of communicating, which remained with me as I learnt to speak, and as my hearing improved. My main influences are my past experiences and all the people I have met on my travels with their own stories.

Robert Sae-Heng

2 **MONDAY** Public holiday, UK, Aus, Can, NZ   2012

3 **TUESDAY**

4 **WEDNESDAY**

5 **THURSDAY**

6 **FRIDAY**

7 **SATURDAY**

8 **SUNDAY**

notes

number nuggets

2007 = the year China overtook the US as the world's biggest carbon-emitting country. But US citizens are still way ahead in individual terms, with 20 tonnes per person per year compared with just 5 tonnes in China.

70 million = the number of Africans likely to be at risk of coastal flooding due to climate change in 2080 (compared with 1 million in 1990).

1 day = the time it takes for the sunlight reaching the earth to provide enough energy to satisfy the world's current power requirements for 8 years.

10.2 kilos = the average amount of chocolate eaten each year by a Swiss person, the highest in the world. The Irish come in third with an annual 8.8 kilos per person.

1 in 47,600 = the lifetime risk of maternal death in Ireland, which makes it the safest country in the world for a woman to give birth. The least safe place is Niger, where the risk is 1 in 7.

10 cents = the average amount Chinese manufacturers receive for their designer clothes from every $1 sale in the US.

60% = the amount of the world's carbon emissions since 1850 produced by just 23 rich countries (who still produce 40% of the current global total).

$607 billion = US military spending in 2008, the last year of the George W Bush presidency – the highest level in real terms since World War Two. The US is responsible for 41.5% of total world military expenditure.

204 million = the number of Muslims living in Indonesia – more than the Muslim populations of Saudi Arabia, Iran, Iraq and Egypt put together.

50 million tonnes = the explosive yield of the largest nuclear weapon ever tested – the Soviet Union's 'Tsar Bomba' in 1961. This compared with the 15,000 tonnes of the bomb dropped on Hiroshima.

$17 billion = the amount lost by the world's two richest men (Warren Buffett from the US and Carlos Slim from Mexico) in the credit crunch. But they still have $38 billion and $37 billion respectively.

700 kg = the average annual amount of carbon dioxide equivalent per person on the planet we would need to get down to in order to meet the IPCC global target for 2050 and avoid the worst effects of climate change. This compares with 1,700 kg for a return flight from London to New York or 3,300 kg for one year's car driving (an average model driven 12,000 km).

$43 billion = the fortune of the world's richest man in 2008, Microsoft mogul Bill Gates (he lost $19 billion in the credit crunch).

$3,581 million = the amount US citizens spend on perfume in a year.

64% = the percentage of Bangladeshi girls married before the age of 18, higher than in any other country.

1 = New Zealand/Aotearoa's ranking in the Global Peace Index, making it the world's most peaceful country. Other reader-country rankings: Canada 8th, Ireland 12th, Switzerland 18th, Australia 19th, Netherlands 22nd, Britain 35th. The US was ranked 83rd of 144 countries, beneath, amongst many others, Peru, Cuba, Senegal, Nepal and Indonesia.

71% = the percentage of births that still go unregistered in the world's least developed countries.

62.7 = the number of homicides per 100,000 people in Colombia, the most dangerous place on earth in this respect, closely followed by Lesotho and South Africa. There are 41 countries with higher murder rates than the US.

49% = the percentage of children in Somalia under 14 engaged in child labour.

51% = the percentage of people in sub-Saharan Africa living below the international poverty line of $1.25 a day in 2005.

29,430 kilowatt hours = the amount of electricity per person used in 2004 in Iceland, the world's biggest per-capita consumer. Reader countries: Canada 18,408; US 14,240; Australia 11,849; NZ/Aotearoa 10,238; Switzerland 8,669; Netherlands 7,196; UK 6,756; Ireland 6,751.

5 = the number of US companies among the world's 6 biggest arms-producing corporations: Boeing; BAE Systems (UK); Lockheed Martin; Northrop Grumman; General Dynamics; Raytheon.

0.968 = Iceland's top rating in the 2008 Human Development Index (HDI), where 1 would be a perfect score. The HDI rates countries not just by income but also by life expectancy, adult literacy and education. Other reader-country rankings: Canada (3rd), Australia (4th), Ireland (5th), Netherlands (6th), Switzerland (10th), US (15th), NZ/Aotearoa (20th), and Britain (21st).

0.329 = Sierra Leone's score in the Human Development Index, the lowest of 179 countries.

metro map – Paris, France

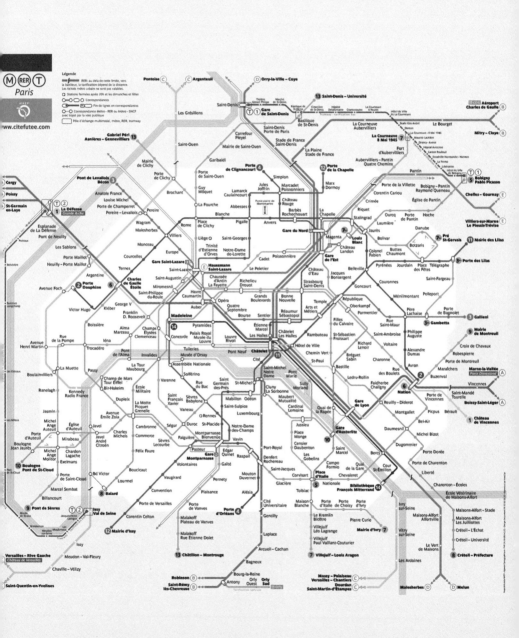

metro map – Barcelona, Spain

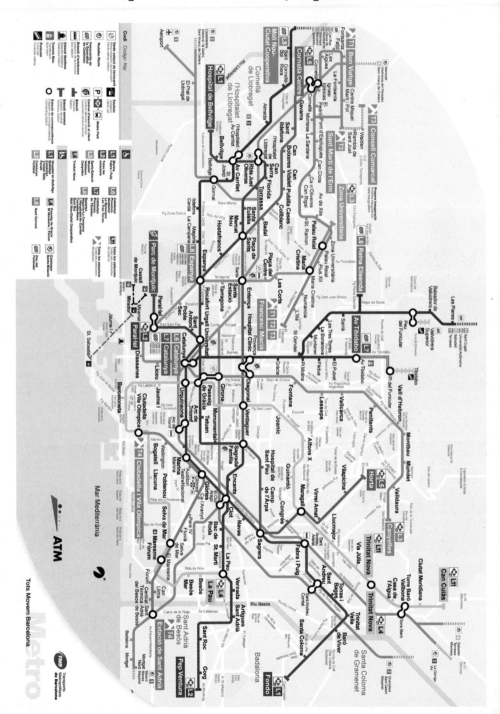

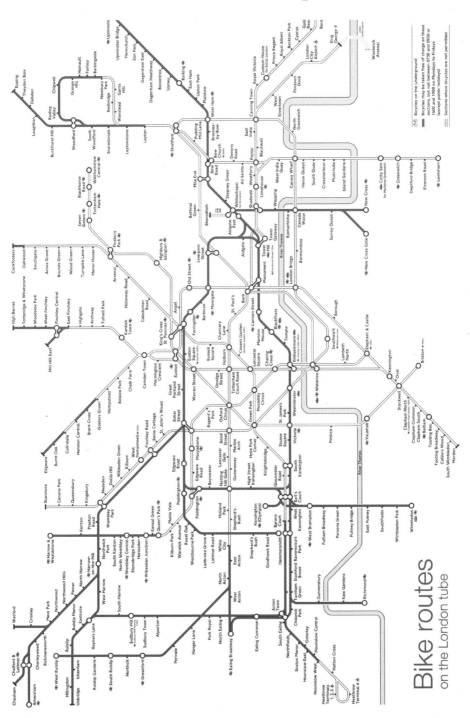

metro map – London, UK

Bike routes
on the London tube

metro map – Amsterdam, Netherlands

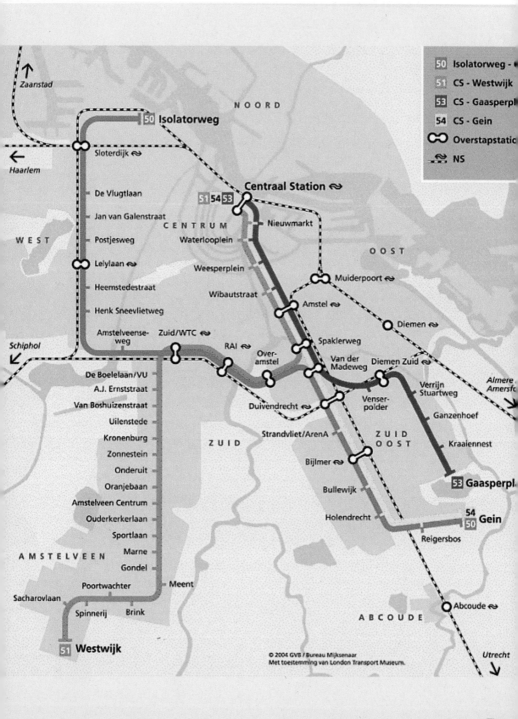

metro map – Sydney, Australia

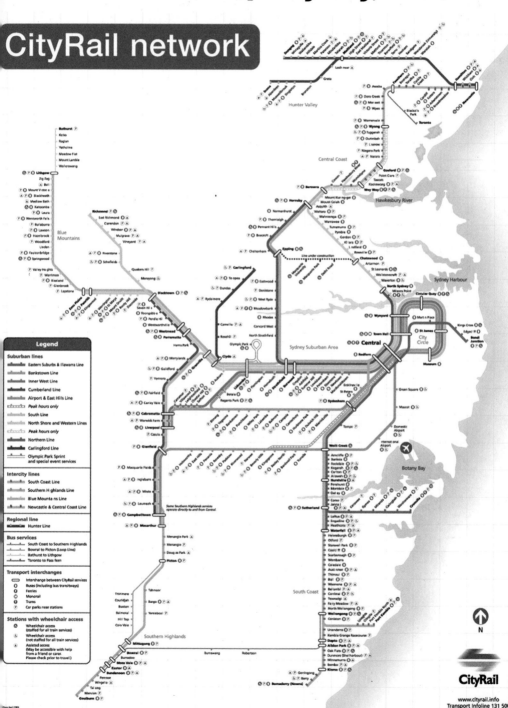

CityRail network

www.cityrail.info
Transport Infoline 131 500

metro map – New York, USA

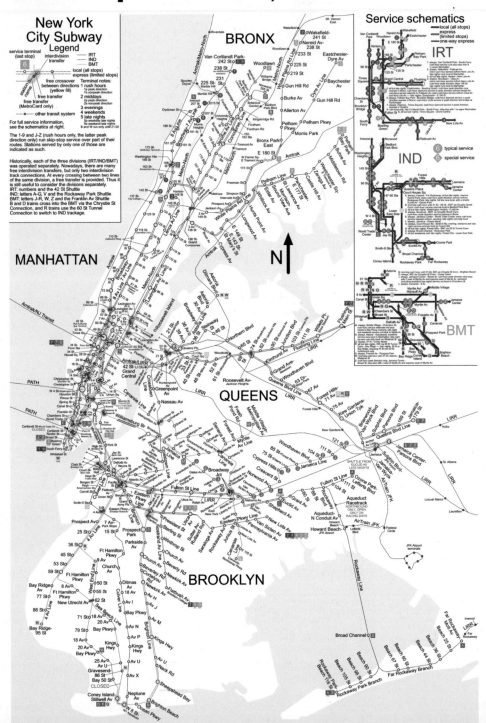

metro map – Moscow, Russia

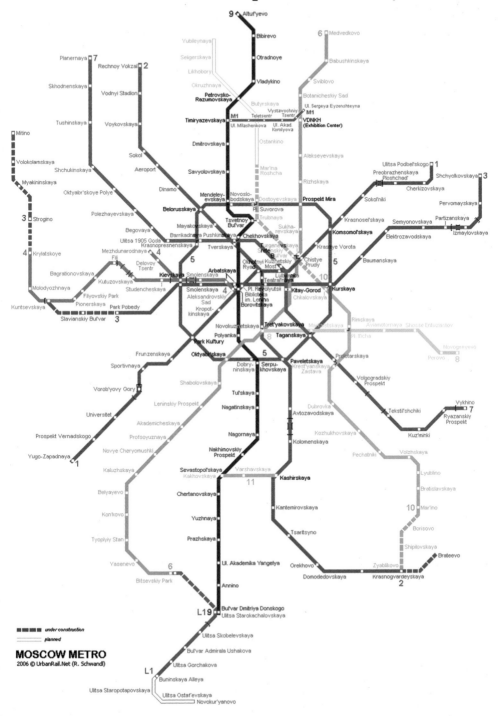

MOSCOW METRO
2006 © UrbanRail.Net (R. Schwandl)

contacts

name

phone

e-mail

web

name

phone

e-mail

web

name

phone

e-mail

web

name

phone

e-mail

web

name

phone

e-mail

web

name

phone

e-mail

web

name

phone

e-mail

web

name

phone

e-mail

web

name

phone

e-mail

web

name

phone

e-mail

web

name

phone

e-mail

web

name

phone

e-mail

web

name

phone

e-mail

web

name

phone

e-mail

web

contacts

name
phone
e-mail
web

name
phone
e-mail
web

name
phone
e-mail
web

name
phone
e-mail
web

name
phone
e-mail
web

name
phone
e-mail
web

name
phone
e-mail
web

name
phone
e-mail
web

name
phone
e-mail
web

name
phone
e-mail
web

name
phone
e-mail
web

name
phone
e-mail
web

name
phone
e-mail
web

name
phone
e-mail
web

credits

Design:
© Ian Nixon / New Internationalist

Photography:
© photographers as indicated

Art and Illustrations:
© artists and illustrators as indicated

Text: © New Internationalist Publications™ Ltd
and artists/individuals as indicated 2011

Printed on recycled paper by C&C Offset Printing Co. Ltd., China,
who hold environmental accreditation ISO 14001.

ISBN: 978-1-906523-35-0

2012 year planner

	JANUARY	FEBRUARY	MARCH	APRIL	MAY	JUNE
MON						
TUE					1	
WED		1			2	
THU		2	1		3	
FRI		3	2		4	1
SAT		4	3		5	2
SUN	1	5	4	1	6	3
MON	2	6	5	2	7	4
TUE	3	7	6	3	8	5
WED	4	8	7	4	9	6
THU	5	9	8	5	10	7
FRI	6	10	9	6	11	8
SAT	7	11	10	7	12	9
SUN	8	12	11	8	13	10
MON	9	13	12	9	14	11
TUE	10	14	13	10	15	12
WED	11	15	14	11	16	13
THU	12	16	15	12	17	14
FRI	13	17	16	13	18	15
SAT	14	18	17	14	19	16
SUN	15	19	18	15	20	17
MON	16	20	19	16	21	18
TUE	17	21	20	17	22	19
WED	18	22	21	18	23	20
THU	19	23	22	19	24	21
FRI	20	24	23	20	25	22
SAT	21	25	24	21	26	23
SUN	22	26	25	22	27	24
MON	23	27	26	23	28	25
TUE	24	28	27	24	29	26
WED	25	29	28	25	30	27
THU	26		29	26	31	28
FRI	27		30	27		29
SAT	28		31	28		30
SUN	29			29		
MON	30			30		
TUE	31					